MW00914832

The Novena to St Philomena: The Wonder-Worker

Fr Peter Mario

Copyright @2024 Fr Peter Mario

Table of Contents

1

Introduction to St. Philomena

The Life and Martyrdom of St. Philomena

St. Philomena, often referred to as "The Wonder-Worker," is one of the most fascinating and enigmatic saints in the Catholic Church. Unlike many saints whose lives are well-documented through historical records or writings, much of what we know about St. Philomena comes from divine revelations and pious tradition. According to these sources, St. Philomena was a young Greek princess who lived during the early centuries of Christianity, possibly during the reign of Emperor Diocletian in the early 4th century.

Her story, as revealed in visions to Sister Maria Luisa di Gesù in the early 19th century, describes a young girl who was deeply committed to her Christian faith. From a very young age, Philomena consecrated her virginity to Christ, a vow she took with utmost seriousness and devotion. This vow would later place her in direct conflict with the Roman authorities.

At the age of 13, Philomena accompanied her parents to Rome to seek a peace agreement with Emperor Diocletian. The emperor, struck by her beauty and charm, offered to marry her, promising her wealth and power. However, Philomena, steadfast in her commitment to Christ, refused his advances, declaring that she was a bride of Christ and could not marry. Enraged by her refusal, Diocletian subjected her to a series of torturous punishments in an attempt to break her will.

Philomena was scourged, yet her wounds were miraculously healed by angels. She was then thrown into the Tiber River with an anchor tied around her neck to drown her, but she was miraculously saved. Finally, the emperor ordered her to be shot with arrows, but even these failed to kill her. Frustrated and determined, Diocletian ordered her beheading, which led to her martyrdom. Throughout her sufferings, Philomena remained resolute in her faith, exhibiting extraordinary courage and unwavering trust in God's providence.

Her martyrdom was not just a testament to her faith but also a powerful symbol of purity, courage, and divine grace. St. Philomena's life, though shrouded in mystery, continues to inspire countless faithful who see in her a model of unwavering faith and purity.

The Discovery of Her Relics

The story of St. Philomena took an intriguing turn in 1802 when her relics were discovered in the ancient Catacombs of Priscilla in Rome. During renovations, a worker uncovered a loculus (a type of small burial niche) sealed with terracotta slabs. On the slabs were inscribed the words "Lumena Pax Tecum Fi" (interpreted as "Peace be with you, Philomena"). Accompanying the inscription were symbols often associated with martyrdom: an anchor, arrows, and a palm.

The discovery of her relics stirred great interest and curiosity among the faithful and clergy alike. After careful examination, the Church concluded that these remains belonged to a young martyr named Philomena, whose death bore the marks of violent persecution. Her remains were transferred to the Church of Our Lady of Grace in Mugnano del Cardinale, Italy, where they remain enshrined to this day.

The transfer of her relics marked the beginning of widespread devotion to St. Philomena. Almost immediately, reports of miraculous healings and divine favors attributed to her intercession began to spread, drawing pilgrims from all over the world. Her relics became a source of immense spiritual and physical healing, and devotion to St. Philomena quickly gained popularity, especially among those seeking cures for illnesses, guidance in times of trouble, and the strength to remain faithful in the face of adversity.

Miracles and Devotions Associated with St. Philomena

The miracles associated with St. Philomena's intercession have been numerous and well-documented, earning her the title of "The Wonder-Worker." One of the most famous miracles occurred shortly after her relics were transferred to Mugnano del Cardinale. A critically ill woman, thought to be at the point of death, was completely healed after invoking St. Philomena's intercession. This miracle set the stage for a series of extraordinary events that would solidify St. Philomena's reputation as a powerful intercessor.

St. John Vianney, the Curé of Ars and a great devotee of St. Philomena, often spoke of her miraculous powers. He attributed many of the miracles in his parish to her intercession, including numerous healings and conversions. St. John Vianney kept a statue of St. Philomena in his parish church and regularly recommended devotion to her, calling her his "dear little saint" and a powerful advocate before God.

Throughout the 19th and 20th centuries, devotion to St. Philomena continued to spread. Many saints, including St. Peter Julian Eymard, St. Madeleine Sophie Barat, and St. Pio of Pietrelcina (Padre Pio), had great devotion to her and testified to her powerful intercession. Her feast day on August 11th is celebrated with special fervor in many parts of the world, particularly in Italy, France, and Latin America.

St. Philomena is often invoked as the patroness

of youth, young people, and those seeking purity. She is also called upon for healing, especially for those suffering from incurable diseases, and for strength in times of temptation or spiritual trial. Her chaplet, consisting of three white beads symbolizing her purity and thirteen red beads commemorating the thirteen years of her life, is a popular devotion among the faithful.

In recent years, devotion to St. Philomena has experienced a resurgence, with many people turning to her for guidance, protection, and healing. Her story, though shrouded in mystery, continues to inspire the faithful to live lives of purity, courage, and unwavering faith in God's providence. Her intercession is sought by those who feel lost or abandoned, those who are suffering, and those who seek to grow closer to Christ.

St. Philomena's life and martyrdom remind us of the power of faith and the strength that comes from total trust in God's will. Her story encourages us to remain steadfast in our commitments, to embrace our crosses with joy, and to believe in the power of prayer and divine intervention. Through her example, we are reminded that no matter how young or seemingly insignificant we may feel, God can work wonders through us if we remain faithful to Him.

St. Philomena's life, martyrdom, and the miraculous discovery of her relics continue to captivate and inspire believers around the world. Her powerful intercession and the countless miracles attributed to her have solidified her status as one of the most beloved saints in the Catholic Church. She stands as a testament to the power of purity, the strength of faith, and the enduring love of God for those who trust in Him completely. As we reflect on her life and devotion, may we be encouraged to deepen our own faith and trust in God's plan for our lives, always seeking to follow the example of St. Philomena, the Wonder-Worker.

2

Understanding Novenas

What is a Novena?

A novena is a powerful and ancient form of

prayer in the Christian tradition, specifically within the Catholic Church, that involves praying for nine consecutive days. The word "novena" is derived from the Latin word "novem," which means "nine." The practice of praying for nine days is deeply rooted in Christian history and scripture, reflecting both a period of waiting and preparation.

The origins of the novena can be traced back to the days following the Ascension of Jesus into heaven when the Apostles and the Blessed Virgin Mary gathered in the Upper Room to pray and await the coming of the Holy Spirit at Pentecost (Acts 1:13-14). This period of nine days of prayer and anticipation is considered the first novena, setting a precedent for future generations of Christians. Over the centuries, the Church has adopted the novena as a formal way of seeking divine intervention, celebrating feasts, or preparing for special occasions.

Novenas are diverse in form and intention. They can be personal or communal, simple or elaborate. Some novenas are dedicated to the Blessed Virgin Mary, such as the Novena to Our Lady of Perpetual Help, while others are dedicated to saints, like the Novena to St. Philomena. Novenas can be prayed for a variety of intentions, including seeking guidance, healing, forgiveness, or specific graces. They are also a common form of preparation for significant liturgical celebrations, such as Christmas or Pentecost.

The Power and Purpose of a Novena

The power of a novena lies in its combination of persistent prayer, faith, and devotion. By committing to pray for nine consecutive days, the individual or community is participating in a spiritual discipline that cultivates patience, trust in God's timing, and a deeper connection to the divine. The repetition of prayer over an extended period allows the faithful to open their hearts more fully to God, to express their needs and desires, and to align themselves with God's will.

One of the key purposes of a novena is to foster a sense of hope and expectancy. When praying a novena, the faithful are reminded of God's faithfulness and are encouraged to trust in His providence. This sense of hope is rooted in the belief that God listens to our prayers and responds in ways that are ultimately for our good, even if the answer is not immediately evident or is different from what we expect.

Novenas also serve as a powerful reminder of the importance of perseverance in prayer. In the Gospel of Luke, Jesus teaches about the value of persistence in the parable of the persistent widow (Luke 18:1-8). Similarly, the act of praying a novena requires a sustained effort, which can deepen the believer's relationship with God and reinforce the importance of continual prayer in daily life.

Moreover, novenas often involve specific prayers, reflections, and petitions that help focus the mind and heart on particular virtues or aspects of the faith. For instance, a novena to St. Philomena may emphasize themes of purity, courage, and trust in divine providence, encouraging the faithful to meditate on these virtues and seek to emulate them in their own lives.

How to Pray a Novena Effectively

Praying a novena effectively involves more than just reciting a set of prayers for nine days. It requires intentionality, focus, and a sincere desire to grow closer to God. Here are some steps and tips to help you pray a novena effectively:

•**Choose Your Novena with Intention**: Begin by selecting a novena that resonates with your current spiritual needs or intentions. It could be a novena to a specific saint whose life and virtues you admire, or it could be for a particular grace or intention, such as healing, guidance, or a special favor.

•**Set a Specific Time and Place for Prayer**: Consistency is key when praying a novena. Choose a specific time each day to pray a novena, and try to stick to it. This helps establish a routine and makes it easier to remember to pray. Additionally, choose a quiet, sacred space where you can focus and minimize distractions, allowing you to be fully present during your prayer time.

•**Prepare Your Heart and Mind:** Before beginning your novena each day, take a moment to quiet your mind and center your thoughts on God. This could involve reading a short scripture passage, taking a few deep breaths, or simply spending a moment in silence, inviting the Holy Spirit to guide your prayer.

•**Pray with Faith and Sincerity**: When praying a novena, approach it with a spirit of faith and trust in God's goodness and mercy. Pray each prayer with sincerity, pouring out your heart to God and expressing your needs, desires, and intentions. Remember that prayer is a conversation with God, and He listens to your heart as much as He hears your words.

•**Reflect and Meditate on Each Day's Prayer**: Many novenas include specific reflections or themes for each day. Take time to meditate on these themes and consider how they apply to your life. Allow the prayers and reflections to deepen your understanding of the virtues and qualities you are seeking to cultivate or the grace you are asking for.

•**Be Open to God's Will**: While praying a novena, it is important to remain open to God's will, trusting that He knows what is best for you, even if it differs from your own desires.

Use the novena as an opportunity to surrender your intentions to God, asking for His guidance and wisdom in all things.

•**Incorporate Other Forms of Devotion**: Enhance your novena by incorporating other forms of devotion, such as attending Mass, receiving the Sacraments, fasting, or performing acts of charity. These additional devotions can enrich your spiritual life and complement your novena prayers.

•**Stay Committed and Persevere**: The commitment to pray for nine consecutive days can be challenging, especially when life gets busy or distractions arise. However, staying committed to your novena is an exercise in perseverance and faith. If you miss a day, do not be discouraged. Simply continue where you left off and trust in God's understanding and grace.

•**Conclude with Gratitude and Trust**: At the end of your novena, take time to thank God for the opportunity to draw closer to Him through prayer. Express your gratitude for His presence in your life and trust that He has heard your prayers. Whether you receive a clear answer to your novena intention or not, trust in God's love and His perfect plan for you.

By following these steps and approaching your novena with faith, sincerity, and perseverance, you can deepen your relationship with God and experience the profound spiritual benefits that come from this beautiful and ancient tradition of prayer. Remember, the true power of a novena lies not just in the repetition of prayers but in the heartfelt connection you build with God through those prayers.

3
The Life and Legacy of St. Philomena

The Patroness of the Youth and the Innocent

St. Philomena has become widely known as the patroness of youth and the innocent, symbolizing purity, faith, and courage in the face of adversity. This title resonates deeply with her story, which, although largely passed down through tradition and revelation, paints a picture of a young girl who remained steadfast in her commitment to Christ despite severe trials and persecution.

As a young virgin martyr, Philomena's life is a compelling example of youthful piety and unwavering faith. From a very early age, she dedicated her life to God, choosing a path of chastity and devotion over worldly comforts and power. Her refusal to renounce her vow to Christ, even under the threat of torture and death by the Roman Emperor Diocletian, illustrates a profound innocence and purity of spirit, qualities that have endeared her to young people and those who seek to live a life of virtue.

Her purity and steadfastness in faith make her an especially powerful intercessor for youth, who often face challenges in maintaining their values in a world that can be full of temptations and pressures. St. Philomena's story encourages young people to stay true to their principles and beliefs, even when doing so might lead to hardship or sacrifice. She serves as a reminder that true strength lies in holding firm to one's faith and moral convictions.

St. Philomena is also a beacon of hope for those who feel oppressed or misunderstood, as her life was marked by misunderstanding and persecution. Her intercession is often sought by those who are wronged, falsely accused, or who face unjust treatment, reflecting her legacy as a protector of the innocent. Her miraculous survival through various tortures before her eventual martyrdom also underscores the belief in divine protection and the triumph of good over evil.

Devotions and Popularity Through the Ages
The devotion to St. Philomena has grown steadily since the discovery of her relics in the Catacombs of Priscilla in Rome in 1802. The early 19th century saw a burgeoning interest in her story as reports of miracles attributed to her intercession began to spread. Her relics, enshrined in the Church of Our Lady of Grace in Mugnano del Cardinale, Italy, became a major pilgrimage site, drawing thousands of faithful who sought healing, spiritual renewal, and divine favors.

One of the most significant contributors to the spread of her devotion was St. John Vianney, the Curé of Ars. He had a profound devotion to St. Philomena, attributing many of the miracles that occurred in his parish to her intercession. St. John Vianney's promotion of St. Philomena played a pivotal role in popularizing her devotion across Europe. He affectionately referred to her as his "dear little saint" and encouraged others to seek her intercession, saying, "To St. Philomena, God refuses nothing."

Throughout the 19th and early 20th centuries,

numerous churches and chapels were dedicated to St. Philomena, and several religious orders adopted her as their patroness. The spread of her devotion was marked by the publication of prayer books, the establishment of confraternities, and the commissioning of statues and icons in her honor. Her chaplet, consisting of thirteen beads to represent the thirteen years she lived, became a popular devotional tool, with each bead representing a prayer of intercession for various intentions.

St. Philomena's popularity extended beyond Europe to the Americas, Asia, and Africa, where many people sought her intercession for healing, guidance, and protection. In many communities, her feast day, celebrated on August 11th, is observed with great enthusiasm, involving processions, Masses, and special prayers. Her story, full of miraculous occurrences and divine interventions, continues to inspire the faithful to this day.

In the modern era, devotion to St. Philomena has experienced a resurgence, particularly among young people and those looking for a model of purity and faith in challenging times.

Her story, though ancient, speaks to contemporary believers about the timeless values of courage, faith, and the power of intercessory prayer. Today, she remains a symbol of hope, purity, and strength, drawing the faithful to her intercession in moments of need and uncertainty.

Testimonies of Miracles and Healings

St. Philomena's legacy is significantly marked by the numerous miracles and healings attributed to her intercession, earning her the title of "The Wonder-Worker." From the moment her relics were enshrined in Mugnano del Cardinale, reports of miraculous cures began to circulate. These accounts range from the healing of physical ailments and diseases to spiritual conversions and resolutions of personal crises.

One of the earliest recorded miracles attributed to St. Philomena occurred shortly after her relics were transferred to Mugnano. A young woman suffering from a severe, life-threatening illness was completely healed after praying for St. Philomena's intercession. This miraculous recovery, considered medically inexplicable, sparked widespread devotion and pilgrimage to her shrine, with many seeking similar miracles.

St. John Vianney also testified to the numerous miracles that occurred in his parish through St. Philomena's intercession. He recounted how the faithful, after seeking her help, experienced miraculous healings from various illnesses, including blindness, paralysis, and even the seemingly impossible healing of cancer. Vianney often encouraged the faithful to place their trust in St. Philomena, citing her powerful intercession as a source of divine grace.

Beyond physical healings, many testimonies speak to the spiritual and emotional healings attributed to St. Philomena. People suffering from deep emotional wounds, addiction, and spiritual dryness have reported experiencing profound peace, renewal of faith, and a renewed sense of purpose after invoking her intercession. Families have testified to restored relationships, individuals to newfound strength in overcoming personal struggles, and communities to a deepened sense of unity and faith.

In more recent times, St. Philomena's

intercession has continued to be sought by those facing seemingly insurmountable challenges. Stories of her miraculous intervention continue to be shared by the faithful worldwide, further cementing her reputation as a saint who responds to the needs of those who seek her help with a sincere heart. Her enduring legacy is one of hope and trust in God's providence, reminding the faithful that no situation is beyond the reach of divine grace and mercy.

St. Philomena’s life and legacy remind us that the power of faith, even in the face of persecution or hardship, can lead to profound transformations and miracles. Her intercession is a testament to the belief that God listens to the prayers of the faithful and that through the saints, the divine is intimately involved in the lives of believers. As a patroness of the young and the innocent, her story continues to inspire and guide those who seek to live lives of purity, courage, and unwavering faith in God's plan.

4

How to Prepare for the Novena

Embarking on a novena is more than just a commitment to a series of prayers over nine days. It's a spiritual journey that involves preparing both your heart and your surroundings to foster a deeper connection with God. Proper preparation can enhance the spiritual experience and help you remain focused and open to receiving God's grace throughout the novena. Here are some guidelines to help you prepare spiritually, create a sacred space for prayer, and incorporate fasting and additional devotions to enrich your novena experience.

Spiritual Preparations

•**Set Your Intentions:** Begin by identifying the intention or specific request you wish to bring before God through this novena. Your intention could be for personal needs, for someone else, for guidance, healing, thanksgiving, or any other matter weighing on your heart. Be clear and concise in your intention, and approach it with humility, understanding that God's will is paramount.

•**Examine Your Conscience**: Reflect on your life and actions, examining your conscience for any areas where you may have strayed from God's path. This process of self-reflection can help you enter the novena with a spirit of repentance and openness. It's also an opportunity to seek the Sacrament of Reconciliation (Confession) before starting the novena, ensuring that your heart is cleansed and ready to receive God's grace.

•**Cultivate a Spirit of Faith and Trust**: Prepare yourself mentally and spiritually by cultivating a deep sense of faith and trust in God. Acknowledge that while you are praying for a particular intention, God knows what is best for you and those you are praying for. Approach the novena with a heart full of faith that God hears your prayers and will respond in His perfect way.

•**Gather Spiritual Resources**: Before beginning the novena, gather any resources you might need, such as prayer books, scripture passages, or devotional readings. Having these materials on hand can help you stay focused and engaged during your prayer time. Additionally, consider reading about the life of the saint to whom the novena is dedicated—in this case, St. Philomena—to better understand their virtues and the context of your prayers.

•**Pray for Guidance from the Holy Spirit**: Invoke the Holy Spirit to guide your thoughts and prayers throughout the novena. Ask for the grace to remain committed, focused, and open to God's will, allowing the Holy Spirit to lead you closer to God each day.

Creating a Sacred Space for Prayer

Creating a sacred space for your novena prayers can help set the tone for a more profound spiritual experience. This space should be a place where you can focus and connect deeply with God, free from distractions and interruptions.

•**Choose a Quiet Location**: Select a place in your home or another location where you can be alone with your thoughts and prayers. This could be a corner of a room, a small table, or even an entire room dedicated to prayer. The key is to find a space where you feel comfortable and can focus without being disturbed.

•**Include Religious Items**: Enhance your sacred space with religious items that inspire and encourage a spirit of prayer. This could include a crucifix, statues or images of saints, a rosary, a Bible, or a prayer candle. For a novena to St. Philomena, consider placing an image or statue of her in your space to help center your focus on her intercession.

•**Use Symbols of Faith**: Adding symbols of faith, such as flowers, incense, or holy water, can help create a more immersive environment for prayer. These symbols can serve as reminders of God's presence and the sacred nature of the novena you are undertaking.

•**Keep It Simple and Focused**: While it's helpful to have religious items and symbols in your sacred space, avoid cluttering it with too many objects. The goal is to create an environment that fosters contemplation and prayer, not to overwhelm the senses. Keep the space simple and focused on helping you connect with God.

•**Maintain a Peaceful Atmosphere**: Ensure that your sacred space is a place of peace and calm. If possible, incorporate soft lighting, such as a candle or a small lamp, to create a warm and inviting atmosphere. Silence or gentle background music, such as Gregorian chants or instrumental hymns, can also enhance your prayer experience.

Suggestions for Fasting and Additional Devotions

Fasting and additional devotions can serve as

powerful compliments to your novena prayers, helping to deepen your spiritual focus and express your devotion to God.

•**Consider a Simple Fast**: Fasting is a time-honored practice in the Christian tradition that involves voluntarily giving up certain foods or meals as a form of penance and spiritual discipline. You could choose to abstain from meat, sweets, or another type of food for the duration of the novena, or fast on specific days, such as the first and last days of the novena. Remember, the purpose of fasting is to draw closer to God, so it should be done with a spirit of humility and sacrifice.

•**Engage in Acts of Charity**: Another way to enrich your novena experience is through acts of charity and kindness. This could involve volunteering your time, helping someone in need, or making a donation to a charitable organization. These acts of service are a tangible way to live out your faith and can help you grow in virtue and compassion.

•**Participate in the Sacraments**: If possible, attend daily Mass or receive the Eucharist during your novena. The Eucharist is a source of great spiritual strength and grace, and participating in this sacrament can enhance your novena prayers. Additionally, frequent Confession is encouraged to maintain a state of grace and spiritual readiness.

•**Incorporate the Rosary or Other Devotions**: Alongside your novena prayers, consider incorporating other devotions such as the Rosary, the Divine Mercy Chaplet, or the Liturgy of the Hours. These devotions can deepen your prayer experience and provide additional opportunities for reflection and spiritual growth.

•**Practice Mindfulness and Meditation**: Take time each day to practice mindfulness and meditation, focusing on God's presence and the intentions of your novena. Spend a few moments in silence, reflecting on the virtues of St. Philomena or the grace you seek, allowing yourself to be fully present in the moment and open to God's guidance.

•**Journal Your Experience**: Keeping a journal throughout your novena can be a meaningful way to track your spiritual journey, note any insights or inspirations, and reflect on how God is working in your life. Writing down your thoughts, prayers, and experiences each day can help you remain focused and committed to the novena.

•**Seek Support from a Spiritual Community**: If possible, share your novena intentions with a prayer group, friends, or family members, inviting them to pray with you or support you in your spiritual journey. A sense of community can provide encouragement and accountability, helping you stay committed to your novena prayers.

By preparing spiritually, creating a sacred space for prayer, and incorporating fasting and additional devotions, you can deepen your novena experience and draw closer to God. Remember that the effectiveness of a novena is not solely in the repetition of prayers but in the sincerity of your heart, your faith in God's providence, and your openness to His will.

5

Novena to St. Philomena

The following novena is designed to deepen your devotion to St. Philomena, reflect on her virtues, and seek her intercession. Each day focuses on a specific theme, encouraging you to meditate on different aspects of her life and faith. Begin each day with an opening prayer, followed by a reflection, scriptural reading, meditation, and closing prayer.

Day 1: The Virtue of Purity

In the name of the Father, and of the Son, and of the Holy Spirit, Amen.

Opening Prayer:
Heavenly Father, as we begin this novena in honor of St. Philomena, we ask for the grace to imitate her virtue of purity. May we always strive to live a life that is pleasing to You. Through her intercession, grant us the strength to resist temptation and remain faithful to Your commandments. Amen.

Reflection:
St. Philomena's commitment to purity was unwavering. Even at a young age, she dedicated her life to Christ, choosing to remain chaste and pure. Her purity was not just physical but also spiritual, rooted in a deep love for God and a desire to serve Him wholeheartedly.

Scriptural Reading:

“Blessed are the pure in heart, for they shall see God.” — Matthew 5:8

Meditation:
Take a few moments to reflect on the importance of purity in your own life. What areas need purification? How can you cultivate a pure heart that seeks God above all else?

Closing Prayer:
St. Philomena, pure and chaste, pray for us. Help us to live in purity of heart and mind, that we may be worthy to see God. Through your powerful intercession, may we grow closer to Him each day. Amen.

In the name of the Father, and of the Son, and of the Holy Spirit, Amen.

Day 2: Courage in Faith

In the name of the Father, and of the Son, and of the Holy Spirit, Amen.

Opening Prayer:
Lord, we thank You for the example of St. Philomena, whose courage in faith inspired many. As we reflect on her life today, grant us the courage to stand firm in our faith, even in the face of adversity. Through her intercession, may we always be bold witnesses of Your love. Amen.

Reflection:
St. Philomena displayed immense courage when she refused to renounce her faith, despite facing severe persecution. Her bravery reminds us that true faith requires strength and courage, especially when confronted with trials and challenges.

Scriptural Reading:
"Be strong and courageous. Do not be afraid; do not be discouraged, for the Lord your God will be with you wherever you go." — Joshua 1:9

Meditation:

Consider the moments in your life when you have been called to show courage in your faith. How did you respond? How can you cultivate greater courage in your relationship with God?

Closing Prayer:

St. Philomena, courageous in faith, pray for us. Help us to be strong and brave in our journey with Christ, trusting that He is always by our side. May your example inspire us to live boldly for Him. Amen.

In the name of the Father, and of the Son, and of the Holy Spirit, Amen.

Day 3: Commitment to God's Will

In the name of the Father, and of the Son, and of the Holy Spirit, Amen.

Opening Prayer:
Gracious God, today we ask for the grace to be fully committed to Your will, just as St. Philomena was. Help us to surrender our own desires and embrace Your divine plan for our lives. Through her intercession, may we find joy in following You. Amen.

Reflection:
St. Philomena's commitment to God's will was unwavering. She chose to dedicate her life entirely to God, even when it meant facing persecution and suffering. Her example encourages us to trust in God's plan for our lives and to remain steadfast in our commitment to His will.

Scriptural Reading:

"Trust in the Lord with all your heart and lean not on your own understanding; in all your ways submit to him, and he will make your paths straight." — Proverbs 3:5-6

Meditation:

Reflect on areas of your life where you find it challenging to submit to God's will. What steps can you take to trust Him more fully?

Closing Prayer:

St. Philomena, committed to God's will, pray for us. Help us to surrender our own plans and embrace God's divine purpose for our lives. May your example guide us in faithful obedience. Amen.

In the name of the Father, and of the Son, and of the Holy Spirit, Amen.

Day 4: Endurance in Trials

In the name of the Father, and of the Son, and of the Holy Spirit, Amen.

Opening Prayer:
Merciful Father, as we reflect on St. Philomena's endurance in trials, grant us the strength to remain faithful during our own times of suffering and difficulty. May we learn from her example and draw closer to You in every challenge we face. Amen.

Reflection:
St. Philomena faced numerous trials with unwavering faith and endurance. Her resilience in the face of suffering teaches us the importance of trusting in God's strength and grace, especially when we encounter hardships.

Scriptural Reading:
"Consider it pure joy, my brothers and sisters, whenever you face trials of many kinds, because you know that the testing of your faith

produces perseverance." — James 1:2-3

Meditation:

Think about a trial you are currently facing or have faced in the past. How did you respond? How can you rely more on God's grace to endure future trials with faith and patience?

Closing Prayer:

St. Philomena, who endured trials with grace and faith, pray for us. Help us to remain steadfast in our own trials, trusting in God's infinite love and mercy. Amen.

In the name of the Father, and of the Son, and of the Holy Spirit, Amen.

Day 5: Trust in Divine Providence

In the name of the Father, and of the Son, and of the Holy Spirit, Amen.

Opening Prayer:
Lord, today we focus on trusting in Your divine providence, just as St. Philomena did throughout her life. Grant us the grace to believe in Your plan for us and to trust that You will provide for all our needs. Amen.

Reflection:
St. Philomena's life was a testament to her trust in God's providence. She believed that God had a plan for her, even in the midst of suffering and persecution. Her faith challenges us to trust in God's goodness and His plan for our lives.

Scriptural Reading:
"And we know that in all things God works for the good of those who love him, who have been called according to his purpose." Romans 8:28

Meditation:
Reflect on a situation where you struggled to trust in God's providence. How can you grow in trusting God's plan and believe that He is working for your good?

Closing Prayer:
St. Philomena, who trusted in divine providence, pray for us. Help us to believe in God's plan and trust that He will provide for all our needs. May your example inspire us to live with faith and confidence in His love. Amen.

In the name of the Father, and of the Son, and of the Holy Spirit, Amen.

Day 6: Embracing Suffering with Joy

In the name of the Father, and of the Son, and of the Holy Spirit, Amen.

Opening Prayer:
Heavenly Father, as we meditate on St. Philomena's joyful acceptance of suffering, help us to embrace our own challenges with a spirit of joy and faith. May we learn to see suffering as a path to greater holiness and a deeper relationship with You. Amen.

Reflection:
St. Philomena embraced her suffering with joy, knowing that it brought her closer to Christ. Her willingness to endure pain for the sake of her faith teaches us the value of seeing suffering as an opportunity for growth and spiritual maturity.

Scriptural Reading:
"I consider that our present sufferings are not worth comparing with the glory that will be

revealed in us." — Romans 8:18

Meditation:
Think about a time when you faced suffering. How did you respond? How can you learn to embrace suffering with a joyful heart, knowing that it brings you closer to God?

Closing Prayer:
St. Philomena, who embraced suffering with joy, pray for us. Help us to see our own sufferings as a path to holiness and to trust in God's plan for our lives. May your example inspire us to bear our crosses with grace and faith. Amen.

In the name of the Father, and of the Son, and of the Holy Spirit, Amen.

Day 7: Devotion to the Blessed Virgin Mary

In the name of the Father, and of the Son, and of the Holy Spirit, Amen.

Opening Prayer:
Loving Father, today we honor St. Philomena's deep devotion to the Blessed Virgin Mary. Help us to grow in our own love for Mary and to seek her intercession in our daily lives. Through her example, may we draw closer to Jesus, her Son. Amen.

Reflection:
St. Philomena had a profound devotion to the Blessed Virgin Mary, recognizing her as a powerful intercessor and a model of perfect discipleship. Her love for Mary teaches us the importance of turning to Our Lady for guidance, comfort, and support in our spiritual journey.

Scriptural Reading:
"Do whatever he tells you." — John 2:5

Meditation:
Reflect on your relationship with the Blessed Virgin Mary. How can you deepen your devotion to her and seek her intercession more frequently in your life?

Closing Prayer:
St. Philomena, devoted to the Blessed Virgin Mary, pray for us. Help us to grow in our love for Mary and to turn to her in times of need. May her example lead us closer to Jesus and inspire us to live as faithful disciples. Amen.

In the name of the Father, and of the Son, and of the Holy Spirit, Amen.

Day 8: Perseverance in Prayer

In the name of the Father, and of the Son, and of the Holy Spirit, Amen.

Opening Prayer:
Eternal God, as we reflect on St. Philomena's perseverance in prayer, grant us the grace to remain faithful in our own prayer lives. Help us to trust in Your timing and to never lose hope in Your promises. Amen.

Reflection:
St. Philomena was known for her perseverance in prayer, consistently seeking God's guidance and strength throughout her life. Her dedication to prayer teaches us the importance of maintaining a strong and consistent prayer life, especially in times of difficulty.

Scriptural Reading:
"Rejoice in hope, be patient in tribulation, be constant in prayer." — Romans 12:12

Meditation:
Consider your own prayer habits. Are there areas where you need to grow in consistency and perseverance? How can you make prayer a more central part of your daily routine?

Closing Prayer:
St. Philomena, who persevered in prayer, pray for us. Help us to remain steadfast in our own prayers, trusting in God's timing and His promises. May your example inspire us to deepen our relationship with God through constant prayer. Amen.

In the name of the Father, and of the Son, and of the Holy Spirit, Amen.

Day 9: Confidence in St. Philomena's Intercession

In the name of the Father, and of the Son, and of the Holy Spirit, Amen.

Opening Prayer:
Almighty God, on this final day of the novena, we place our trust in the powerful intercession of St. Philomena. Grant us the confidence to approach her with our needs and to believe in her ability to intercede on our behalf. Amen.

Reflection:
Throughout the ages, countless miracles have been attributed to the intercession of St. Philomena. Her powerful prayers have brought healing, comfort, and guidance to many. Today, we are reminded of the importance of seeking her intercession with confidence and faith.

Scriptural Reading:
"Therefore I tell you, whatever you ask in prayer, believe that you have received it, and it will be yours." — Mark 11:24

Meditation:
Reflect on your belief in the power of intercession. Do you trust in the saints' ability to pray for you and assist you in your spiritual journey? How can you grow in confidence in seeking St. Philomena's intercession?

Closing Prayer:
St. Philomena, powerful with God, pray for us. We ask for your intercession today and every day, trusting that you will bring our needs before the throne of God. May your prayers obtain for us the graces we seek and draw us closer to Christ. Amen.

This novena offers a structured approach to prayer, meditation, and reflection on the life and virtues of St. Philomena. By focusing on a different aspect of her spiritual journey each day, you can deepen your devotion to this remarkable saint and grow closer to God.

In the name of the Father, and of the Son, and of the Holy Spirit, Amen.

Daily Prayers and Reflections

Daily Prayers and Reflections for the Novena to St. Philomena
Incorporate these daily prayers and reflections to deepen your spiritual journey during the Novena to St. Philomena. Begin each day with a Morning Prayer to set the tone for your day, followed by an Evening Prayer to reflect on your day and the day's theme. Each day also includes a unique reflection to meditate on St. Philomena's virtues and how they can be applied to your life.

Morning Prayer
Heavenly Father, as I begin this new day, I turn to You with a heart full of gratitude. I thank You for the gift of life, the grace of this novena, and the example of St. Philomena, whose faith and purity inspire me. As I dedicate this day to You, help me to live according to Your will and to embody the virtues that St. Philomena so beautifully exemplified. Grant me the courage to face any challenges with faith, the patience to

endure trials with hope, and the love to serve others with joy. Through the intercession of St. Philomena, may I grow closer to You in all I do today. Amen.

Evening Prayer
Loving God, as the day draws to a close, I come before You to offer my thanks for Your countless blessings. I thank You for guiding me through the day and for the moments of grace that have drawn me closer to You. I reflect on the virtue of St. Philomena that I have meditated upon today. Help me to internalize these lessons and to apply them in my daily life. Forgive me for the times I may have faltered, and strengthen me to begin anew tomorrow. Through the powerful intercession of St. Philomena, I pray for Your continued guidance and protection. Amen.

Reflections for Each Day of the Novena

Day 1: The Virtue of Purity

Reflection:
Reflect on the significance of purity in your life. Purity is not only about chastity but also about purity of intention, thought, and action. Consider how you can live with a pure heart, free from malice, deceit, and sin. St. Philomena's commitment to purity was a testament to her love for God and her desire to live a life pleasing to Him. How can you cultivate this same purity in your thoughts, words, and deeds?

Day 2: Courage in Faith

Reflection:
Consider the moments in your life where you have been called to show courage in your faith. Courage in faith means standing firm in your beliefs, even when it is difficult or unpopular. Reflect on the courage of St. Philomena, who faced persecution and suffering with unwavering faith. How can you show courage in your daily life, especially when faced with challenges or adversity?

Day 3: Commitment to God's Will

Reflection:
Reflect on the concept of surrendering to God's will. St. Philomena's life was marked by her deep commitment to God's plan, even when it meant suffering. Contemplate the areas in your life where you may be struggling to surrender fully to God's will. How can you trust more in His divine plan, even when it is not what you would have chosen for yourself?

Day 4: Endurance in Trials

Reflection:
Reflect on your own experiences of trials and difficulties. St. Philomena endured great suffering with faith and patience, trusting in God's grace to see her through. How do you respond when you face trials? Do you turn to God for strength, or do you rely on your own strength? Consider how you can cultivate greater endurance and trust in God during times of difficulty.

Day 5: Trust in Divine Providence

Reflection:

Reflect on the concept of trusting in God's providence. St. Philomena's life exemplifies a deep trust in God's care and provision, even in the most challenging circumstances. Consider how you can grow in your trust in God, believing that He is working for your good, even when you cannot see the full picture. How can you surrender your worries and anxieties to God, trusting that He will provide for all your needs?

Day 6: Embracing Suffering with Joy

Reflection:

Reflect on the idea of embracing suffering with joy. St. Philomena faced her sufferings with a spirit of joy and hope, knowing that they were a path to greater holiness. How do you respond to suffering in your own life? Do you see it as a punishment or an opportunity for growth? Consider how you can cultivate a spirit of joy, even in the midst of suffering, trusting that God is using it to bring about something good.

Day 7: Devotion to the Blessed Virgin Mary

Reflection:
Reflect on your devotion to the Blessed Virgin Mary. St. Philomena had a deep love for Mary, turning to her for guidance, comfort, and intercession. Consider how you can grow in your devotion to Mary, seeking her help in your own spiritual journey. How can you imitate her example of perfect discipleship and surrender to God's will?

Day 8: Perseverance in Prayer

Reflection:
Reflect on the importance of perseverance in prayer. St. Philomena was known for her steadfastness in prayer, even when it seemed like her prayers were not being answered. Consider how you can grow in your commitment to prayer, trusting that God hears you and will answer in His perfect timing. How can you develop a more consistent and faithful prayer life, regardless of the circumstances?

Day 9: Confidence in St. Philomena's Intercession

Reflection:

Reflect on the power of intercession. St. Philomena's intercession has brought about countless miracles and answered prayers. Consider the areas in your life where you need her help. How can you approach her with confidence, trusting in her powerful intercession before God? How can you cultivate a deeper trust in the communion of saints and their ability to intercede on your behalf?

By incorporating these daily prayers and reflections into your novena, you can deepen your spiritual journey and grow closer to St. Philomena. Each day's focus encourages you to reflect on different virtues and aspects of your faith, helping you to draw closer to God and become more like St. Philomena in your own life.

7

Additional Prayers to St. Philomena

In addition to the novena prayers, the following

additional prayers can enhance your devotion to St. Philomena and seek her powerful intercession for various needs and intentions.

Litany of St. Philomena
Lord, have mercy on us.
Christ, have mercy on us.
Lord, have mercy on us.

Christ, hear us.
Christ, graciously hear us.

God the Father of Heaven,
Have mercy on us.
God the Son, Redeemer of the world,
Have mercy on us.
God the Holy Spirit,
Have mercy on us.
Holy Trinity, one God,
Have mercy on us.

Holy Mary, Mother of God,
Pray for us.
St. Philomena,
Pray for us.
St. Philomena, filled with divine grace,
Pray for us.

St. Philomena, chosen from your infancy by the Sacred Heart of Jesus,
Pray for us.
St. Philomena, beloved daughter of Jesus and Mary,
Pray for us.
St. Philomena, who by your faith and fortitude triumphed over all trials,
Pray for us.
St. Philomena, who by your purity and chastity shone like a lily among thorns,
Pray for us.
St. Philomena, who endured martyrdom with patience and joy,
Pray for us.
St. Philomena, who performed miracles by the power of God,
Pray for us.
St. Philomena, who intercedes powerfully for those in need,
Pray for us.

Lamb of God, who takes away the sins of the world,
Spare us, O Lord.
Lamb of God, who takes away the sins of the world,

Graciously hear us, O Lord.
Lamb of God, who takes away the sins of the world,
Have mercy on us.

Pray for us, St. Philomena,
That we may be made worthy of the promises of Christ.

Let us pray:
O God, who showered Your servant, St. Philomena, with the gifts of grace and virtue, grant that we may imitate her example and be strengthened by her intercession. Through Christ our Lord. Amen.

Chaplet of St. Philomena

Introduction:

Begin with the following prayer:
"O St. Philomena, Virgin and Martyr, you are a shining example of purity and courage. Through your intercession, we ask for the grace to live with the same devotion to God. We pray that you guide us and help us to overcome the trials

of this life. Amen."

Chaplet:

On the large beads (or the Our Father beads):
"St. Philomena, pray for us."

On the small beads (or the Hail Mary beads):
"St. Philomena, assist us in our needs."

Concluding Prayer:
"O glorious St. Philomena, who did suffer so much for the love of Christ and whose intercession has brought healing and miracles to so many, we entrust to you our needs and intentions. Obtain for us the grace to follow your example of faith and courage. May we live our lives with purity and dedication to God. Through Christ our Lord. Amen."

Consecration to St. Philomena

Consecration Prayer:
"O St. Philomena, we consecrate ourselves to you, body and soul, and pledge to follow your example of virtue and dedication to God. We ask for your powerful intercession to help us

grow in holiness and to overcome the challenges we face. By your prayers, help us to remain steadfast in our faith and to live a life pleasing to God. We place all our hopes and needs in your hands, trusting in your care and protection. Through Christ our Lord. Amen."

Prayer for Special Intentions

"O St. Philomena, powerful intercessor and patroness of the youth and the innocent, we come to you with our special intentions and needs. We place before you our petitions and ask for your powerful intercession before the throne of God. Please intercede for us, especially in (mention your specific request or intention), and obtain for us the graces we need. Through your example and your prayers, may we be strengthened in our faith and trust in God's loving providence. We ask this through Christ our Lord. Amen."

These additional prayers and devotions can deepen your relationship with St. Philomena and invoke her intercession for your needs and intentions. Incorporating these prayers into your daily routine can enhance your spiritual growth and provide additional support during your novena.

8

Testimonies and Miracles

Modern-Day Miracles of St. Philomena

St. Philomena has been known for centuries as a powerful intercessor, with numerous miracles attributed to her prayers. In recent times, there have been many reports of miraculous healings and extraordinary interventions through her intercession. These modern-day miracles further affirm her role as a devoted and powerful saint.

Some notable examples include:

•**Healing of Serious Illnesses**: Many devotees have reported miraculous recoveries from severe illnesses after invoking St. Philomena's intercession. Medical conditions that seemed hopeless have seen unexpected turnarounds.

•**Resolution of Financial Difficulties**: St. Philomena has been invoked by those facing financial crises. There are accounts of sudden and unexpected financial aid that has come through after prayers to her.

•Restoration of Broken Relationships: Families and relationships that were strained or broken have experienced reconciliation and healing through St. Philomena's intercession.

These testimonies showcase her continued presence and active role in the lives of her devotees, illustrating the power of her intercession in contemporary times.

Personal Testimonies from Devotees

Personal testimonies are powerful affirmations of faith and can offer hope and encouragement to others. Here are a few examples from those who have experienced the intercession of St. Philomena:

•Testimony of Maria, a Mother: "I prayed to St. Philomena during a particularly difficult time when my daughter was facing a serious illness. After fervently asking for her intercession, my daughter's condition began to improve dramatically. I am forever grateful for St. Philomena's help."

•**Testimony of John, a Young Professional**: "Facing a major career setback, I felt lost and hopeless. I turned to St. Philomena in prayer, asking for guidance and help. Remarkably, opportunities began to open up, and I was able to turn my situation around. I believe St. Philomena played a significant role in this transformation."

•**Testimony of Elizabeth, a Student**: "While struggling with exams and academic pressure, I asked St. Philomena for strength and clarity. I felt a sense of calm and focus, and my performance improved significantly. I attribute this to the intercession of St. Philomena."

These stories reflect the tangible impact of St. Philomena's intercession in various aspects of life, inspiring others to seek her help with faith and trust.

Sharing personal experiences of St. Philomena's intercession can be a source of inspiration and encouragement for others. Your story can offer hope to those in need of reassurance and strengthen the faith of fellow believers.

9
Conclusion

Final Thoughts on Devotion to St. Philomena
St. Philomena's life and legacy offer a profound example of faith, purity, and perseverance. Her intercession has continued to touch the lives of many, both historically and in modern times. Embracing her virtues and seeking her intercession can lead to a deeper spiritual life and a stronger connection with God.

Encouragement for Continued Prayer and Devotion
As you conclude this novena, remember that devotion to St. Philomena is not limited to the duration of the novena. Continue to seek her intercession in your daily life, cultivating a lasting relationship with this beloved saint. Regular prayer and reflection on her virtues can enrich your spiritual journey and bring you closer to God.

Appendix

Relevant Scripture Readings

•**1 Peter 5:10:** "And after you have suffered for a little while, the God of all grace, who has called you to his eternal glory in Christ, will himself restore, confirm, strengthen, and establish you."

•**Hebrews 12:1-2**: "Therefore, since we are surrounded by so great a cloud of witnesses, let us also lay aside every weight, and sin which clings so closely, and let us run with endurance the race that is set before us, looking to Jesus, the founder and perfecter of our faith."

Made in the USA
Thornton, CO
11/15/24 23:59:38

70732d12-1df2-4433-8052-bf649a11a310R01